The Life and of Thomas Hardy

by Ben Harwood

Published by: *Inspiring Places Publishing*
2 Down Lodge Close
Alderholt
Fordingbridge
SP63JA
ISBN 978-0-9564104-0-5

Printed by Corvette Printing Ltd., Bournemouth

Other titles by *Inspiring Places Publishing:*

Fossils and Rocks of the Jurassic Coast

The Jurassic Coast - Illustrated

Ancient Dorset

Dark Age Dorset

Historic Dorset

Mysterious Places of Dorset

Smugglers' Dorset

Mystery Big Cats of Dorset

Day Tours in the East of Dorset

Buy online at: www.inspiringplaces.co.uk

Front cover photograph: Thomas Hardy aged 21, © Dorset County Museum
Back cover photograph: The Turbeville window in Bere Regis church,
honouring the ancient family that Hardy used in Tess of the D'Urbervilles.
First page: Hardy with bicycle, © Dorset County Museum
Right: Bere Regis church

Contents

Note: The book is illustrated with pictures of places associated with Hardy and with his works.

Introduction

Thomas Hardy's popularity as an author has declined little in the one hundred and thirty-five years since the publication of *Far from the Madding Crowd*, a notion supported by the ongoing adaptation of his novels for other media, most notably the 2009 BBC television series, *Tess*. The charm with which Hardy recounts the lives of the inhabitants of the area he named 'Wessex' seemingly continues to hold appeal for each new generation of readers, combining as he does the pastoral, comedic and tragic in a way that seems as natural as the backdrop to the novels, the countryside of southern England. It is not difficult to see why this is the case: when one reads Hardy, it is near impossible not to find something rewarding or to your taste, be it his engagement with crucial social issues, his unwaveringly accurate depiction of Nature, and the symbolic importance it holds within the stories, the comedy, the emotion and character that brim from each page, even his unusual choice of the tragic novel (only Flaubert can be said to have done the same with distinction). In this book I hope to illuminate aspects of Hardy's novels and poems that will lend an increased enjoyment and awareness to the reading of them, and perhaps encourage those of you who have not yet done so to immerse yourself in Hardy's Wessex and its inhabitants, or thumb a collection of his poems.

Right: Hardy's cottage at Higher Bockhampton, now owned by the National Trust and open to the public. This is where he was born and grew up. Hardy lived here until he was 34 and wrote "Under the Greenwood Tree" and "Far from the Madding Crowd" here.

Left: Hardy's heart is buried in this grave in Stinsford churchyard with Emma, his first wife. On page 7 is pictured Stinsford Church where Hardy's father and grandfather played in the church choir.

Brief Biography

Hardy was born on the 2nd June, 1840 in a cottage in Higher Bockhampton, near Dorchester, to Thomas and Jemima Hardy. His father was a stonemason and builder, but his mother, a well read and educated woman, taught the young Thomas at home until he went to school at eight years old, famously giving him a copy of Virgil on his twelfth birthday. His early years were spent in close contact with both Nature and the rural way of life, leaving an indelible trace on the young boy, evident in all his writing. He left education aged sixteen, becoming apprenticed to the Dorchester architect John Hicks. This architectural training was to prove a formative and important aspect of Hardy's youth, permeating, as it does, the whole of Hardy's canon. He continued his apprenticeship by moving to London in 1862 to work with Arthur Blomfield, moving back home after five years as Hicks' assistant. It was this year that Hardy began his first (unpublished and lost) novel, *The Poor Man and the Lady*.

Three years later, on an architectural visit to the church of St. Juliot in Cornwall, he met his future wife, Emma Lavinia Gifford. Though culminating in an ultimately unhappy marriage, the romance between Hardy and the rector's sister-in-law was a passionate one. They married in 1874, and by then Hardy had written and published four novels, allowing him to retire from architecture and earn his living solely as a writer.

In 1885, after a brief and unsuccessful foray into the London literary scene, Hardy moved into Max Gate, just outside Dorchester. Hardy himself designed the house, and it proved to be his home for the rest of his life. From that year to the publication of *Jude the Obscure* in 1895, Hardy wrote four of his most famous novels: *The Mayor of Casterbridge, The Woodlanders, Tess of the D'Urbervilles,* and the aforementioned *Jude*. After one more novel, *The Well Beloved*, Hardy abandoned novels altogether, and concentrated on the poetry he had been writing since the mid-1850s.

In 1912, after a lengthy estrangement and growing ill health, Emma died at Max Gate. The effect of her death on Hardy surprised even himself, and his poetry of 1912-13, reminiscing on Emma's death as well as happier times, is generally regarded as some of his best. However, in 1914, he married a close friend, Florence Dugdale, who, despite Hardy's clear attachment to the memory of Emma, cared assiduously and lovingly for him up until his death on 11th January 1928. Interestingly, though Hardy desired for his body to be buried next to Emma's grave in the parish graveyard in Stinsford, there was a huge public call for him to be buried in Poets' Corner in Westminster Abbey. Eventually a compromise was reached, and, perhaps most fittingly of all, Hardy's ashes were interred in Westminster, but his heart was buried next to Emma at Stinsford.

Influences

With a writer as unique and prolific as Hardy, the question arises, 'How exactly did Hardy's unique style and mode develop from his upbringing'? What were the formative influences for him as a writer? This is a difficult question, as unlike many other writers, there are no real precedents for his type of writing - indeed, the novel had been (and still to a point is) considered an exclusively comic medium, and so for Hardy to use it as a vehicle for (to quote Lord David Cecil) such "exceptionally tragic" stories as *Tess* and *Jude*, presents the investigator with something of a literary puzzle.

As such, the clearest and most important influences on Hardy seem to lie outside the literary sphere. Hardy's affinity with Nature [i.e. the rural landscape], evidenced in nigh on every piece of his writing, plays a larger and more crucial part in his work than most other novelists and poets. It has been noted many times that Nature is considered as much of a 'character' as any of the human populace of each novel. But leaving Nature's influence in each novel at that - the mere identification of a featureless presence against whose permanence man's transitory birth, glimmer and fading is played out - does not, I believe, provide a satisfactory account of Nature's importance in Hardy's work. It does indeed take on human forms and characteristics, such as the "sigh of the immense sad soul" of the surroundings in chapter four of *Tess*, but the so called permanence of Nature is one that is threatened by the introduction of agricultural machinery to the farming process. Man's own impermanence and vulnerability are not just contrasted with Nature's grand steadfastness; they are almost echoed by it.

In a similar way, the 'rustics' of his novels occupy an unchanging position, summarising events, emphasising the human element of the story, and providing some light relief in the tradition of a Trinculo or Dogberry. Their existence, seemingly as an immortal whole, transcends (or at least underpins) the fleeting drama of the main characters. Whilst ostensibly human as individuals, the rustics are present in each novel, immoveable and yet, unlike Nature, vulnerable. For instance, in *Under the Greenwood Tree*, a band of capable yet endearingly rural musicians are about to be replaced at the parish church by an organ. Again, the natural order of country life is threatened by the introduction of the modern. This uncanny parallel between man and Nature emphasises the connection between the two that Hardy so clearly perceived.

Hardy's youth in Dorset undoubtedly provided more than a grain of inspiration: his mother's educated and loving influence is reflected in his portrayal of women such as Tess, Sue Bridehead and Bathsheba Everdene; women who buck the trend of the 'domestic angel' of Victorian fancy, and who are strikingly independent in a male dominated society. The curiously prominent yet discreet smuggling business was a crucial part of Dorset's economy during the early nineteenth century, and his short story, "The Distracted Preacher", playfully acknowledges the moral dilemma that faced locals when they came into contact with these smugglers. The idea is that a local preacher falls in love with a beautiful young woman, who turns out to be a smuggler. Unsure whether to turn her in to the authorities as a responsible citizen, or to turn a blind eye, allow the local economy to carry on undisturbed, and continue his relationship with her, the intriguing and irreverent depiction of a preacher shows Hardy at his best; considering real moral issues, but tempering the drama with humour and love. But, I believe, the most important influence on his writing from the world around him stemmed simply from the nature of a small, rural village, and the hardships people had to face, day in, day out. Lord David Cecil in his book, Hardy the Novelist, points this out very succinctly and powerfully:

" Tragedy was not confined to ballads...dramas arising from the narrow poverty-stricken circumstances in which its inhabitants lived. Lovers were parted: a young man, in need of a livelihood, would leave the place to seek his fortune; years later he would return, to find his sweetheart married to another. In such a world, confined and elemental, passions grew to obsessions...Hardy saw two hangings before he was eighteen."

"Confined and elemental" are perhaps two of the most appropriate words one can use to describe Hardy's novels, and indeed his poems: in Michael Henchard (*The Mayor of Casterbridge*) we have, perhaps, an absolute and definitive illustration of those two qualities in one man!

While it seems as though Hardy's main influences came (interestingly) from outside literature, digging a little deeper rewards us with a certain less crucial, but nonetheless tangible grasp of Hardy's literary predecessors or influences. As I have mentioned before, Hardy was given a copy of *Virgil* on his twelfth birthday, and this affinity with the classics can be seen quite clearly through the presence of: the rustics, who most definitely resemble a chorus in a Greek drama; the tragedy of character, defined by Aristotle, which locates the cause of a tragedy as a minor but fatal flaw in the hero or heroine - such as Henchard's pride; and the frequent, though generally inappropriately clumsy, classical references that litter the novels.

As with almost every great late Victorian writer, the publication of *The Origin of Species* must have influenced Hardy to some degree. His early crisis of faith, noted in Ralph Pite's excellent biography, *Thomas Hardy: The Guarded Life*, caused by Darwin's ostensible deicide, is reflected in his perception of life being ultimately random and without design. This sentiment is beautifully expressed in his poem, "Hap" (1866):

> *If but some vengeful god would call to me*
> *From up the sky, and laugh: "Thou suffering thing,*
> *Know that thy sorrow is my ecstasy,*
> *That thy love's loss is my hate's profiting!"*
>
> *Then would I bear, and clench myself, and die,*
> *Steeled by the sense of ire unmerited;*
> *Half-eased, too, that a Powerfuller than I*
> *Had willed and meted me the tears I shed.*
>
> *But not so. How arrives it joy lies slain,*
> *And why unblooms the best hope ever sown?*
> *--Crass Casualty obstructs the sun and rain,*
> *And dicing Time for gladness casts a moan....*
> *These purblind Doomsters had as readily strown*
> *Blisses about my pilgrimage as pain.*

Hardy also, it would appear, found other contemporary inspiration. The bildungsroman (German, literally meaning 'novel of formation') is a type of novel made popular by the German enlightenment, and sees the main character grow physically and spiritually from child to adulthood. Whilst Hardy does not adhere rigidly to all the principles of the bildungsroman (it traditionally ends with the main character being accommodated into society after a long and arduous journey of clashes between social obligations and individual desires), *Jude the Obscure* offers us Hardy's closest model of it. *Tess* and *The Mayor of Casterbridge*, his other two 'tragedies of character', also to some extent appropriate this form, both however leaving us with what is more accurately described as a *thwarted* bildungsroman. Noting this then immediately suggests the possibility of that then (and now) giant of English fiction, Charles Dickens, being an influence on Hardy. Some of Dickens' most famous novels, *David Copperfield*, *Oliver Twist* and *Great Expectations*, use the style and shape of the bildungsroman, and the popularity of Dickens seems likely to have permeated through the ether to Hardy's consciousness, voluntarily or involuntarily.

Below: Woolbridge Manor, where Tess and Angel spent their wedding night. It was originally the home of the Turbeville family; Hardy found much inspiration from the history and legends of "Wessex".

Hardy and the Novel

Rather than launching headlong into Hardy's work itself, I think that if we provide ourselves with a background from which to come at his work, the significance and merit of his work will be much clearer. In short, I propose first to look at Hardy and the novel, and then Hardy and his novels.

Perhaps the most unusual feature of Hardy's novels, most especially the later ones, is how they deal unflinchingly with tragedy. The so-called tragedies of character, encompassing *The Mayor of Casterbridge*, *Tess of the D'Urbervilles* and *Jude the Obscure*, are, without doubt, tragedies (as the name would suggest). This may not seem remarkable upon first viewing; these novels have been absorbed into the very fabric of our culture, so familiar are they. However, when one discovers, or remembers, that the novel has, since its genesis, been considered an almost exclusively comic form, the unrelenting inevitability of each character's tragedy chimes awkwardly with received ideas of the novel.

While what exactly constitutes the 'first novel' is unlikely ever to be agreed, it began really to take hold of the public interest in the eighteenth century, when writers such as Daniel Defoe, Henry Fielding and Jonathan Swift (to name but three) began to rise to prominence with works such as *Robinson Crusoe*, *Tom Jones* and *Gulliver's Travels* respectively. For a considerable amount of time, the novel was generally considered to be a frivolous form of writing, and less 'intellectual' than poetry or drama. This was reflected in the way some novelists (Defoe and Samuel Richardson in particular) presented their work as true memoirs or histories, so as to lend a certain credibility to the work. Fielding, on the other hand, openly admitted to fabricating his plots. The idea of the novel as a comic vehicle was perpetuated by writers such as Dickens and Austen in the nineteenth century, and it wasn't really until the end of the nineteenth century that the novel was reconsidered as a 'serious' art form, Henry James and George Eliot most notably expanding its scope.

This artistic prejudice (right or wrong) dates right back to ancient Greece, where Aristotle in his *Poetics* asserts that tragedy "is a dramatic, not a narrative form." In using the novel as the medium in which to narrate his tragedies of character, Hardy was breaking with literally hundreds, if not thousands of years of tradition, and it is important to keep this in mind when reading the novels.

The key question that then arises is whether or not he is successful in marrying tragedy and the novel. Obviously, in some sense, compelling evidence for his success comes from merely looking at the sales figures of his books; however, the same criteria would also lead to favourable judgement on Dan Brown, Andy McNab and Chris Ryan, and so perhaps it is better to look at the question in a more direct, textually involved way.

Ian Watt, in his book *The Rise of the Novel,* helpfully outlines the guiding principles of the novel. Arising more from trial and error than a conscious manifesto of ideas, these are the six practices that best describe the novel's position in literature, if not its appeal as well:

It deals with low life. That is not meant in a derogatory sense; it means that, unlike supposedly 'serious' drama or poetry, its subjects did not have to be gods, kings and beautiful princesses. It portrayed and existed in as many different social levels as the author saw fit. A perfect example of this is Daniel Defoe's eponymous and morally dubious heroine from the novel Moll Flanders. It is also quite emphatically true of Hardy, dealing as he does with Tess the milkmaid, Jude the stonemason, and Francis Troy the soldier and ladies' man, to name but three.

According with this new freedom the novel also boasts an absence of formal convention. Rather than having to work within the strict confines that had previously guided metre and rhyme in poetry and drama, the nature of the novel meant that it could, to a certain extent, do away with these conventions, and allow the author to express himself (at least in theory) more freely.

Once more, this leads to another tenet; the originality of plot. Because of the absence of formal conventions, the author did not have to choose a story from mythology and treat it as he would to get the best out of it - he, or she, were free to construct their own plot and characters, again helping to liberate literature from the shackles of classical conventions and rules.

Fourthly, the novel is characterised by a particularity of character and location. By this I mean that the novel often focuses its attentions on one character or place, allowing the reader a rich and nuanced understanding of either or both.

This is generally achieved by offering the reader 'exhaustive presentation, rather than fine concentration', where, rather than trying to condense an emotion or scene into a few lines of poetry, a description of a landscape can last for as long as is needed to convey exactly what the author feels.

Lastly, it is written in a plain, understandable style. There is no necessity for high-flown rhetoric, and ingenious sentence construction; the writer can express his or her ideas in writing in the same manner as he or she might speak them.

Are these qualities which could theoretically work well with tragedy? The first tenet, that of dealing with all social classes, seems to fit in very well with Hardy's particular brand of rural tragedy. At the time when Hardy started writing, the traditional agricultural community was under serious threat from new machinery and the allure of the rapidly expanding cities. Machines such as the thresher in *Tess* (which is presented by Hardy as an instrument of punishment on the heroine) were rapidly replacing traditional farm hands. These hands had something of a nomadic profession, moving around from one farm to the next, depending on what seasonal work needed to be done, and so great unrest was caused by the new machines, making them effectively redundant.

'The Swing Riots' of October to December 1830 were the workers' response to the continued reduction in wages and underemployment. They consisted mainly of rioting in places perceived to be connected with the farmers (workhouses and tithe barns, for example), rick burning, the destruction of threshing machines, and, even in some cases, the maiming of cattle. The figurehead of the riots was a widely adopted pseudonym: Captain Swing. Letters, often of a threatening tone, were sent to land owners and newspapers under this name, the first being reported in The Times on October 21, 1831. It is clear that more than one person used this pseudonym, as the letters differ wildly in style and levels of literacy, but there is no doubt that the name offered a banner for displaced and unemployed agricultural workers to rally to. All in all, six hundred rioters were imprisoned, five hundred deported, and nineteen executed.

The riots are a perfect example of the civil unrest caused by the modernisation of farming, and though they occurred twelve years before Hardy was even born, their reverberations would no doubt have been felt by the young author: as I have mentioned, in *Tess*, our eponymous heroine is forced to work on top of the dangerous thresher by Farmer Groby as revenge for being knocked down by Angel earlier in the book. The connection with 'The Swing Riots' does not just end there. Captain Swing provides very definite and morbid connotations of the punishment for one involved in the riots, and it is difficult to ignore that Tess' own end is prefigured by the name.

Hardy's awareness of the plight of the agricultural classes is evident throughout his work, particularly in the lament for the reddleman at the beginning of *The Return of the Native,* which indicates a poignant sadness at the loss of traditional occupations:

"The traveller with the cart was a reddleman - a person whose vocation it was to supply farmers with redding for their sheep. He was one of a class rapidly becoming extinct in Wessex, filling at present in the rural world the place which, during the last century, the dodo occupied in the world of animals. He is a curious, interesting, and nearly perished link between obsolete forms of life and those which generally prevail."

It seems as though Hardy is fighting to be the ideal detached, objective observer that an omniscient narrator should be, and is yet unable to restrain his own elemental passions and emotions when narrating. "Curious," and "interesting" give a hint of Hardy trying to adopt an unemotional facade, which is then brought crashing down by the bitterness and wistfulness so evident in "nearly perished" and "obsolete." The 'tragedy of the working classes', so evident in many later Victorian novels and poetry, is, in Hardy, more the 'tragedy of the agricultural working classes', utilising the novel's ability to deal with different social backgrounds.

The absence of formal conventions in the novel, I believe, helps Hardy update tragedy, by removing the necessity of investing the heroes or heroines with certain key virtues. Hardy's main characters, whom the tragedies befall, are not one and the same. You could not place Jude Fawley in the place of Michael Henchard and produce the same novel. This is one of the advantages the novel has over the majority of previous dramatic tragedies.

An originality of plot is partly what makes this the case. Tragedies, particularly tragedies in verse, of the eighteenth century have not proved to be of an enduring interest to audiences. Part of this is likely to have been due to the rigid adherence to Classical rules that was so prevalent at the time; playwrights were not encouraged to engage in writing plots or characters that uniquely suited their needs. Instead, they called upon myths and legends to provide both, and while some of the greatest works of literature have been based on legends and myths, Hardy's fresh approach to tragedy (interestingly) coincided with the revival of drama in the second half of the nineteenth century. The freedom that Hardy could use because he wrote novels allowed his stories to proceed as he wanted: the main characters could bump into past acquaintances in inopportune times as many times as Hardy deemed necessary and could be inadvertently thrust upon hard times whenever Hardy wanted; the whole cast could enter and exit as he saw fit.

However, many academics and critics find it difficult to swallow some parts of the stories. The events seem just a little bit too providential or unlucky, the coincidences a little too contrived, so that they struggle to take them seriously. I shall consider these claims later when dealing more closely with the novels themselves. It is undoubtedly true, however, that total freedom with the plot may not, in all cases, result in a superior story. There must be a reason why the classical plots have endured so long and nourished so many texts.

Hardy's tragedies again seem to suit the next characteristic of the novel, that of a particularity of location and character. The boon that this afforded Hardy is evident even in the titles of his novels: *The Mayor of Casterbridge: The Life and Death of a Man of Character* shows Hardy's intention to deal specifically with both one character in particular, and the particular character of that person. The wording seems curiously appropriate to Hardy's novels. Not only does Hardy deal with the character of characters, but locations also have their own characters. Hardy's locations are not the painted, static backdrop of a theatre: they are living and breathing, witness to all the events in the area, simultaneously inheriting and emanating the history of the land to all around them. It is partially Hardy's acute awareness of the particularity of location and character required for proper tragedy that makes his novels so successful. Having Tess, whose character all along seemed doomed by her own nature, captured at Stonehenge illustrates this. Stonehenge was, and still is, looked on with a mystical regard for the pagan past, and so, as Tess is arrested for finally putting Angel, herself and their love before the values and morals imposed by a Christian society (I will discuss this later in more detail), Stonehenge reminds us of a time before the dominance of Christianity. It reminds the reader of the permanence of truly human values, not ones imposed by the Church. Indeed, it is most symbolic that Tess acknowledges her guilt for an act of murder in a specifically *non-Christian* setting. Stonehenge infiltrates the consciousness of the reader, taking him or her, in a small way, outside their time of reading, just as Hardy's use of the name Wessex recalls the old Anglo-Saxon kingdom.

It is also not just Hardy's awareness of physical location, but also temporal location, where they are in time. Though *Far from the Madding Crowd* is set seemingly in the present (though of course its exact temporality remains ambiguous), Hardy's description of Weatherbury as being at least fifty years behind the cities in developmental terms transports the tragi-comedy out of the contemporary, back to a time before the reign of Victoria, before the Industrial Revolution. In doing this, Hardy banishes the hulking, faceless presence of machines and factories, as a result bringing human drama to the foreground, making the lives and actions of these individuals far more important and moving than they would be, were the primary concerns of the characters grain production or the new threshing machine.

Hardy clearly makes the most of the novel's ability to hold the magnifying glass, as it were, over one character or location - each tragedy is a result of nuances in the characters' dispositions and their interaction with their surroundings. Their actions would often be inexplicably ludicrous if we were not familiar with their character.

In stark contrast to his poems, Hardy's novels offer exhaustive presentation, rather than fine concentration. Whereas his poems rarely exceed six or so stanzas, most of his novels comply with the Victorian tradition for long (or at least reasonably long) fiction. It could, perhaps, be said that, were we to consider Hardy's works as tapestries, the poems would hold up a magnifying glass to each thread, whereas the novels would reveal a wider picture of the whole. This proclivity of the novel has, perhaps unsurprisingly, positive and negative aspects when applied to tragedy. It could allow the novelist to portray every nuance and event leading up to the culminating tragedy, helping to better explain the tragedy itself. However, it could also suffer from a lack of conciseness, and a consequent slackening of the dramatic tension. On the one hand, Tess' adherence to her own moral code, not the church's, does not make sense without full knowledge of her life and her character, but, in spreading out the tragedy over four hundred-odd pages, does Hardy dissipate the essence or concentrate of the tragedy? Naturally, that is something that every reader must decide for himself/herself, but I believe that the book itself is not the only factor to consider when deciding this. If, for instance, one spreads out the reading of the book itself over weeks or even months, the tragedy will feel less substantial or concentrated. But if one reads the book in a few concentrated sittings, or simply keeps in mind the previous parts of the book whilst reading, there is no need for the novel to feel stretched or weak.

Being written in the *plain style*, both roots the novel in more widely accessible literary soil, and begins to explain its popularity. Its main function in the tragic novel seems to be to make the tragedy as a whole more realistic, more earthy - closer to common speech. Hardy's use of dialect in particular stands out as appealing to all spheres of life, while his frequent classical references extend a welcoming hand to the educated classes. The novel allows this because of its plain style: dialect is allowed entry into literature through the novel, and classical references that were obscure or unmarked in poetry and drama can be flagged up and explained in the novel in simple, understandable language.

Opposite page: Looking across the Blackmore Vale from Bulbarrow Hill.
In *Tess of the D'Urbervilles* Hardy describes this scene:

*This fertile and sheltered tract of country, in which the fields are never brown
and the springs never dry, is bounded on the south by the bold chalk ridge that
embraces the prominences of Hambledon Hill, Bulbarrow, Nettlecombe-Tout,
Dogbury, High Stoy, and Bubb Down. The traveller from the coast, who, after
plodding northward for a score of miles over calcareous downs and corn-lands,
suddenly reaches the verge of one of these escarpments, is surprised and delighted
to behold, extended like a map beneath him, a country differing absolutely from
that which he has passed through. Behind him the hills are open, the sun blazes
down upon fields so large as to give an unenclosed character to the landscape,
the lanes are white, the hedges low and plashed, the atmosphere colourless.
Here, in the valley, the world seems to be constructed upon a smaller and more
delicate scale; the fields are mere paddocks, so reduced that from this height their
hedgerows appear a network of dark green threads overspreading the paler green
of the grass. The atmosphere beneath is languorous, and is so tinged with azure
that what artists call the middle distance partakes also of that hue, while the
horizon beyond is of the deepest ultramarine. Arable lands are few and limited;
with but slight exceptions the prospect is a broad rich mass of grass and trees,
mantling minor hills and dales within the major. Such is the Vale of Blackmoor.*

Bulbarrow and other chalk prominences were favourite places of Hardy; he
writes about them in his poem "Wessex Heights".

> *There are some heights in Wessex, shaped as if by a kindly hand
> For thinking, dreaming, dying on, and at crises when I stand,
> Say, on Ingpen Beacon eastward, or on Wylls-Neck westwardly,
> I seem where I was before my birth, and after death may be.*
>
> .
> .
>
> *So I am found on Ingpen Beacon, or on Wylls-Neck to the west,
> Or else on homely Bulbarrow, or little Pilsdon Crest,
> Where men have never cared to haunt, nor women have walked with me,
> And ghosts then keep their distance; and I know some liberty.*
>
> *[first and last stanzas]*

The Novels

While theoretical discussions over the suitability of the novel as a tragic medium are key to an understanding of Hardy's work, there is undoubtedly a danger in deciding what elements of the novel should fit with tragedy before we read the books themselves. We, the reader, might find that the parts of the novel we expected to perfectly suit the tragic actually jar horribly with the dominant feel of the book. Bearing this in mind, we now move on to the books themselves.

Hardy undoubtedly has his characters in full view throughout his novels; their concerns are his concerns. But, if one takes a closer look at how they are actually portrayed, we find that rather than giving us a full description of the characters' appearances, Hardy instead describes them by first of all colouring in their surroundings. He illustrates his characters by offering us a character-shaped silhouette, with all the descriptive detail on the outside of the shape. It is the external forces which shape, mould and build the characters, not just their own natures. *The Mayor of Casterbridge: The Life and Death of a Man of Character* illustrates this perfectly. Though, in my opinion, it is Hardy's finest study of character, the idea of an actual character is a notion that is slippery and difficult to grasp in his books. We are introduced to Henchard and his wife and child on the first page, but the detail is only superficial - what they are wearing mainly. It takes three pages for either of them to utter a word, and yet Hardy has already started forming and manipulating our impressions of them. "The man was of a fine figure, swarthy, and stern in aspect," and from that we are already drawing what conclusions we will, though nothing has actually been said about his character or nature. As Penelope Vigar points out, Hardy's drawing of character is most similar to the chiaroscuro effect in painting. This is where the painter uses extremes of dark and light to emphasise certain parts of the painting. In a similar way, Hardy obscures and highlights certain parts of the scene or character, rather than shining a full beam of authorial light to illuminate all aspects of the story. Reading the novels with this in mind makes for fascinating reading, and, by observing what the author chooses to show and what not to show, gain a real insight into the author's intentions.

That Hardy chooses not to say certain things about certain characters is proven by the number of times that we physically shout at Tess to not do whatever she is about to do. Hardy never lets her do what we would do in the same situation; he does not even entertain the possibilities. As a result we only see the decision we ourselves would not make - all other options are obscured, shaded out, and Tess' actions are made to seem an inevitable result of the situation. Here, in obscuring and not mentioning the way for Tess to live a happy life, Hardy illustrates the hopelessness of Tess' situation; the fact that she cannot simply 'be' with Angel when he comes back, and the result of her family's dependency on Alec.

Looking at Tess, one then may begin to become aware of Hardy's women. There is no doubt that they divide opinion, something that would have been especially true of their reception at the time of publication. Many Victorians envisaged womankind at their best as 'domestic angels'; paragons of virtue and integrity, unflinchingly supporting their husbands. Though submissive, they were certainly acknowledged as being of critical importance to the man.

Hardy's women rarely fit into this category, and this can perhaps be traced back to his mother, Jemima, who home schooled him from a young age before he went to school. Accounts of her register her as educated and well read. No doubt the powerful female presence in his early life prevented Hardy from allowing 'domestic angels' to penetrate his novels. Women like Tess Durbeyfield, Bathsheba Everdene, even Fancy Day, from *Under the Greenwood Tree*, assert their femininity, as well as their right to behave as men would. Tess obviously does not behave according to the ordinary moral principles of the time; Bathsheba takes on her uncle's old farm flying in the face of nearly everyone's opinion that it was not a job for a woman; Fancy Day also does not behave as a 'domestic angel', despite her angelic appearance, in promising her hand in marriage to two different men.

However, Hardy's heroines are not just immoral or controversial for the sake of provoking discussion: they do not simply make rash decisions because they are women. They are put in situations whereby they can do nothing else but what they do. Most of the time they are put there by men, consciously or inadvertently, and then are vilified for their subsequent actions. There is no doubt that Hardy intended to show this when writing the novels, and therefore he can be considered, I believe, as a minor, but important campaigner for women's rights.

Many critics have been disappointed by Hardy's manipulation of plot so as to procure the ending he desires. It has been called clumsy, over calculating, and even unbelievable. Are we really supposed to believe that Tess would murder Alec before running away with Angel, when they had the chance to live a happier life? Would Susan Bridehead really have left Jude for Richard Phillotson? These turning points of the plot offer to many readers a barrier which blocks their enjoyment of the novel. David Cecil sees nothing previously in either of their natures which suggests an explanation for their subsequent actions, and so regards the novels ultimately with suspicion and hesitation. However, in reality, I feel that Hardy not only offers the reader a reasonable explanation, but also centres one of the main themes of both books around these actions. The issue that I believe Hardy is addressing is that of the bind between woman and man. Hardy surely would have been painfully aware of this thanks to his increasingly difficult and isolating marriage with Emma Gifford.

In Tess, Hardy portrays the dominant, even crippling oppression of accepted moral standards over natural human instinct. These moral standards ostracise Tess, eventually leading to her death. It is her sense of obligation to her father which makes her take the goods to market the morning after he drinks himself into a stupor, accidentally killing the horse as she does so. It is the same sense, combined with pressure from her mother, that makes Tess travel to their (impostor) relatives, and so on and so forth. We see that there is little else Tess could have done - or at least, Hardy hopes us to. The problem arises when Tess tells Angel of her previous sexual experience, and he, because of accepted moral values, refuses to join himself to Tess. Her fears are then realised - Angel changes completely from the loving and infinitely forgiving fiance to a harbinger of unrelenting and near-sighted moral ethics. She sees God rejecting her a second time (after the priest refuses to bury her child in consecrated ground). When Angel comes back, it is too late. All Tess sees is the same choice as was offered last time, which only led to tragedy. To be with Angel, she must make herself, in effect, a "widow". Surely, because of all that has gone before, there can only be one way to be with Angel?

Jude presents a similar situation, but in this case, the institution that keeps the two lovers apart is that of marriage, and this time it is on both sides. Jude foolishly binds himself to Arabella and Sue marries Mr Phillotson. When the two do cohabit, again they face unassailable difficulties; being shunned by everyone they meet, as well as caring for Jude's boy by Arabella, Little Father Time. Eventually, the remnant of Jude's first, socially proper marriage breaks apart his marriage to Sue, his true love, and thus accepted moral standards literally break apart Jude's immoral but spiritual marriage to another woman. After all this, Sue sees it as the work of God - a God she previously could not believe in - and takes the death of her children as a sign that she should return to her original, 'sinless' marriage. At this heartrending and climactic moment, Jude and Sue spell out what Hardy is trying to say throughout the book:

Above: The Cross and Hand near Batcombe. Probably a Roman pillar used as some sort of boundary marker, it has been associated with various legends. It was here that Tess met Alec and where he made her promise never to tempt him again. Hardy used a number of ancient legends in his works; he also remembers a different legend here in his poem "The Lost Pyx".

"'I have made up my mind that I am not your wife! I belong to him. I sacramentally joined myself to him for life. Nothing can alter it.'
'But surely we are man and wife, if ever two people were in this world? Nature's own marriage it is, unquestionably!'
'But not Heaven's. Another was made for me there, and ratified eternally in the church at Melchester.'"

We see here the frightening, and, as Hardy would see it, ludicrous idea that a prior claim on one person is forever binding, though that person may find a true partner, and that acting out of the interests of everyone involved, annulling the first, unsatisfactory bind, and being with the one you love, is immoral.

Perhaps, though, Hardy is saying something slightly more subtle, or maybe even failing to come to a judgement at all. Phillotson did love and still loved Sue throughout, though she loved Jude; so, do two people's happiness take precedence over one's? Should Sue have obeyed her instinct and her own nature, and been with Jude, no matter what the consequences, or should she honour the promise she made first of all, sacrificing her own and Jude's happiness for that of another? It is a question without a definitive answer, but it is interesting to remember that Hardy, after the death of Emma, married a close friend, Florence Dugdale, only two years after her death.

Whatever Hardy was saying in these two novels, many did not like or agree with it. Indeed, the public reaction to Jude caused Hardy to concentrate solely on poetry for the remaining thirty or so years of his life. However, despite it often being claimed that *Jude the Obscure* was his last published novel, the last was, in actual fact, *The Well-Beloved*, published in 1897, and set on the fictional 'Isle of Slingers' - a version of the Isle of Portland.

Right: Ackling Dyke, possibly the best preserved Roman road in southern England. "The Roman Road" sets a stark contrast between history and memory, and in this opposition lies the key to the poem. Hardy appropriates the grandeur of the past to suit an intimate and homely memory. The poem focusses on the human present through the lens of impersonal history.

The Roman Road runs straight and bare
As the pale parting-line in hair
Across the heath. And thoughtful men
Contrast its days of Now and Then,
And delve, and measure, and compare;

Visioning on the vacant air
Helmeted legionnaires, who proudly rear
The Eagle, as they pace again
The Roman Road.

But no tall brass-helmeted legionnaire
Haunts it for me. Uprises there
A mother's form upon my ken,
Guiding my infant steps, as when
We walked that ancient thoroughfare,
The Roman Road.

Poetry

It is important to recognise that Hardy considered himself first and foremost a poet. Hardy wrote poetry well before he was published as a novelist, but his first volume, *Wessex Poems*, only came out in 1898. Having seen Hardy's last novel, *The Well-Beloved*, in terms of new work, the British public were then exposed solely to Hardy the poet until his death in 1928. Though Hardy's poems are unquestionably dissimilar to his novels, the *atmosphere* and *tone* of the poems still remain uniquely his own.

It would be somewhat optimistic to attempt a comprehensive survey of Hardy's poems, such was the output of the man. Even surveying a certain period of his writing could well prove too vast, as well as not giving an accurate portrayal of his canon. With this in mind, what I hope the following section will do is to use a small number of poems - representative, hopefully, of some common themes and images in his work - to illustrate a few ways of engaging with his poetry that might throw up a few surprises. As well as getting a sense of his poetry in comparison to his other poems and his novels, I will also try and look at the words on the page themselves. This way, the reader may gain some confidence to encounter and tackle any other poem of Hardy's that they may come across with vigour, enthusiasm and insight that are all their own. With luck, as well, the attentive reader might pick up on ideas, imagery or linguistic features that I have left out even in the poems below. What follows is not a 'guide' or 'walkthrough' for each poem; it is, I would like to think, something perhaps parallel to the primary 'meaning' of the poem (if such a thing does indeed exist!), but that is nonetheless interesting. In other words, my aim here is to provide the fishing rod, rather than fish.

"On a Midsummer Eve" gives, for me, an intimate and representative sense of Hardy's poetry.

I idly cut a parsley stalk,
And blew therein towards the moon;
I had not thought what ghosts would walk
With shivering footsteps to my tune.

I went, and knelt, and scooped my hand
As if to drink, into the brook,
And a faint figure seemed to stand
Above me, with a bygone look.

I lipped rough rhymes of chance, not choice,
I thought not what my words might be;
There came into my ear a voice
That turned a tenderer verse for me.

Besides the poem showing Hardy something more disturbing on this extraordinary night (see *A Midsummer Night's Dream*) than ordinary superstition would suggest, in this poem I believe there exists a microcosm of Hardy's work. Initially, with characteristic understatement and effortlessness, Hardy begins his work in Nature; the parsley stalk, and then contemplates the connection between it, himself and the greater, cosmic perspective, in blowing it 'towards the moon'. This has echoes of his novel, *Two on a Tower*, and the observatory that affords the characters a glimpse of that which is infinitely grander than the characters themselves. This concern with the grand, cosmic perspective seems thoroughly in keeping with Hardy's view on the role of 'Chance' or 'Happenstance' in life, emphasising, as it does, our lack of significance in this world.

The ghosts that "would walk with shivering footsteps towards the moon" provide an interesting notion - one perhaps more applicable to modern literary theory than a nineteenth century novelist, but nonetheless, it is worth mentioning. The idea goes that 'ghosts' are ever-present in literature, be it ghosts of the author's memories and experiences, ghosts of the voices of other authors, ghosts of characters and events from within the text. It is these ghosts, so the theory suggests, that shape the text, and mould it into what it becomes. It then proposes that, in the text, the reader can perceive these ghosts, and that it is even one of the crucial elements of reading. In the poem Hardy almost seems to recognise the unconscious nature of the production of these ghosts in literature, saying, as he does, that he "had not thought what ghosts would walk."

Throughout the poem, as I will try to show, very nearly each line offers the keen and observant reader a thought or a point of engagement with Hardy's writing and even literature in general. Though picking apart each line to the minutest detail would yield some fruitful but dry rewards, now is perhaps not quite the appropriate time. Nonetheless, it would be remiss not to pay any attention to these moments. For instance, the second stanza (or paragraph), containing the words "as if to drink," and "a faint figure," seems to remind the reader of the unreal and mimetic quality of writing itself. Writing is not real life - only a figurative representation of it, a *faint*, unreal image. By the very nature of writing, it cannot be any more than a representation, and Hardy here, consciously or unconsciously, is recognising this.

Whilst Hardy seems to represent the process of writing, he also, in his own words, gives us a description of his poetry in a perfectly Hardy-esque manner; "rough rhymes of chance, not choice." It would be difficult to argue that Hardy as a writer was the kind of perfectionist craftsman who knew exactly where each word needed to go. Much of his writing seems to carry an indefinable attraction for readers - something vague and yet commanding in its effect on us - and it feels as if this is the case even within the poem. A perfectionist craftsman certainly would not have started the poem with "I idly," the reading out of it is too awkward and does not sit well on the tongue. However, the "shivering footsteps" and "bygone look" reach out and pull in the reader's undefined feelings. The voice that "turned a tenderer verse" is equally interesting, as there appears to be nothing for "tenderer" to compare itself against. Tenderer than what? Here again one feels that Hardy is referencing his own poems, in particular his poems about his first wife, Emma, and the tenderer bent that his thoughts took after her death. However, these thoughts are merely some ideas with which to start looking at the poem, and there is much more to be found and enjoyed within it.

Perhaps unsurprisingly, Hardy's poetry, as well as containing a self-reflexive aspect, also deals with the connection between man and Nature. "The Fallow Deer at the Lonely House" offers a slight shift in perspective to Hardy's usual method of portraying this connection:

> *One without looks in to-night*
> *Through the curtain-chink*
> *From the sheet of glistening white;*
> *One without looks in to-night*
> *As we sit and think*
> *By the fender-brink.*

> *We do not discern those eyes*
> *Watching in the snow;*
> *Lit by lamps of rosy dyes*
> *We do not discern those eyes*
> *Wondering, aglow,*
> *Fourfooted, tiptoe.*

Rather than offer us an image of how man is connected to Nature, Hardy in this poem seems to offer an image of Nature trying to connect with man. "One without looks in tonight" immediately separates Nature and man, but seemingly with Nature looking in. This is not a perspective that is often present in his writing; Nature appears omnipresent, permeating every character's actions. However, this time Nature is not as intrinsically present in our lives as before, and while Hardy is aware of the view that Nature has of us, "we do not discern those eyes."

This connection is also evident in a curious manner in Hardy's poem "The Convergence on the Twain (Lines on the loss of the 'Titanic')", written, as the name suggests, after the loss of the 'Titanic'. In it the iceberg is animated by Hardy's pen, and shown as a machination of 'The Immanent Will', Hardy's term for the random workings of fate or 'Hap':

> "*The Immanent Will that stirs and urges everything*
> *Prepared a sinister mate*
> *For her - so gaily great -*
> *A Shape of Ice.*"

Though the workings of 'The Immanent Will' are indeed random, the poem conveys a very definite sense of a connection between the two:

> "*...As the smart ship grew...*
> *...In shadowy silent distance grew the Iceberg too.*"

The two, as the poem later states, are 'intimately welded' together in their respective futures; man and Nature coming together inexorably and (in a manner befitting Hardy) with tragic consequences. As the reader may have picked up on already, either directly from the writing or from this book, the circumstances brought about by 'The Immanent Will' are rarely happy ones. *The Mayor of Casterbridge* gives us both ends of the spectrum; Henchard's tragic and terrible last will and testament, and the happiness of Elizabeth-Jane. Yet, she seems curiously unmoved by the whole thing, and the whole thing appears almost as a joke; Elizabeth-Jane happens to end up happily, Henchard happens to die miserably, but does her happiness ease our anguish at Henchard's demise? Not at all. What is, I believe, most interesting about the poem is that it raises the question of whether or not Hardy considered 'The Immanent Will' to be a part of Nature, or separate from it, and subject to the same chance happenings as ourselves. In the poem Hardy seems to separate Nature and 'Hap' with the line "The

The coast of north Cornwall where Hardy explored with Emma [right] whilst working on St. Juliot's church. Below is the poem "Beeny Cliff", written after Emma's death. The poem is an example of a place or monument evoking an intense emotional response from Hardy, triggering sentiments that, whilst not necessarily long-buried, create a sense of rediscovery for the reader.

O the opal and the sapphire of that wandering western sea,
And the woman riding high above with bright hair flapping free-
The woman whom I loved so, and who loyally loved me.

The pale mews plained below us, and the waves seemed far away
In a nether sky, engrossed in saying their ceaseless babbling say,
As we laughed light-heartedly aloft on that clear-sunned March day.

A little cloud then cloaked us, and there flew an irised rain,
And the Atlantic dyed its levels with a dull misfeatured stain,
And then the sun burst out again, and purples prinked the main.

Still in all its chasmal beauty bulks old Beeny to the sky,
And shall she and I not go there once again now March is nigh,
And the sweet things said in that March say anew there by and by?

What if still in chasmal beauty looms that wild weird western shore,
The woman now is-elsewhere-whom the ambling pony bore,
And nor knows nor cares for Beeny, and will laugh there nevermore.

Immanent Will...prepared a sinister mate," which places Nature under the yoke of Fate. However, the iceberg is, without doubt, an agent of 'The Immanent Will', and so must it not be part of it? This question is one that is not answered definitively, nor in isolation, and each reader may come to a different conclusion on it. Nevertheless, it is an interesting and important question.

Apart from "The Convergence of the Twain", and, as mentioned earlier, "Hap", there are relatively few poems dealing directly with 'The Immanent Will' in Hardy's canon. Strange, given that it forms the basis for each of his novels! Whilst, as with life itself, it is ever-present, permeating each action and reaction, Happenstance seems to take a backseat in the poetry, particularly in collections of what is often deemed his 'best' work. What is present in the poetry that is not so much in the novels, however, is a more self-reflexive willingness (or even need) to write about and consider himself through verse. Whilst certain novels of his were seemingly based on his experiences and thoughts - most notably Hardy's troubled marriage in *Jude* - they seldom revealed much about the author himself. His poems, on the other hand, deal repeatedly and candidly with his own memories, experiences, regrets and thoughts.

Most famous of this more personal style of writing is his volume "Poems 1912-1913" which primarily deal with his then recently deceased wife, Emma. These poems have a stinging poignancy to them, with or without knowledge of the state of their marriage when Emma died, but what is also noteworthy is the way that Hardy attempts to deal with the loss, and the subtleties and nuances of Hardy's suffering.

Primarily, Hardy seems to find some kind of comfort or release in juxtaposing the past and the present. It is something that many do in the face of grief or bereavement, and so perhaps it is not surprising. If anything, it increases the appeal of the poems, coming from a common ground of human experience and action, not a realm of poetic fancy.

There are plenty of beautiful poems from that collection showing a real sorrow at Emma's passing, and grief at his treatment of her. For instance, the first stanza of "Your Last Drive" gives us an eloquent sense of Hardy's sentiments in a typically bleak and dramatic way:

"Here by the moorway you returned,
And saw the borough lights ahead
That lit your face - all undiscerned
To be in a week the face of the dead,

And you told of the charm of that haloed view
That never again would beam on you."

As I have mentioned, the reader finds Hardy reflecting on a
past event, and contrasting it with its impossibility in the present. This
sentiment, a universally recognisable one as I have suggested before, is
further transformed into the realms of the all-embracing by describing
Emma's face as "the face of the dead." Not just *a* face of the dead, but
the face. The poem, as with all of Hardy's about Emma, is undoubtedly
beautiful, but just what about it makes it so beautiful is, again, as with a
majority of his writing, difficult to ascertain. Perhaps - and one can only
speculate, as each reader will obviously have a different idea of beauty - part
of the beauty can be found in the way Hardy uses contrasting images to
create (literally in this case!) shades of light and dark. I have mentioned
this previously when talking about the novels and how Hardy illustrates
his characters not just by painting them outright in bold and distinctive
colours, instead obscuring and revealing certain parts of each scene or
person. This technique has much in common with the style of painting
known as *chiaroscuro*, most famously utilised by Caravaggio, whereby the
artist uses extremes of light and dark to reveal or hide what he chooses to.
It is a mode of illustration, I believe, that adds a certain delicate beauty to a
scene, as well as a definite sense of drama and occasion (something Hardy
no doubt desired).

Yet, despite these poems and their immediate beauty, there lies within
them - or at least some of them -a note of Hardy the stubborn, unrepentant,
misanthrope. For instance, in "The Voice", Hardy, though he describes
himself:

"Thus I; faltering forward,
Leaves around me falling,"

also says that Emma - *"woman much missed-"* calls to him now, saying that
she is not now as she was.

"Woman much missed, how you call to me, call to me,
Saying that now you are not as you were
When you had changed from the one who was all to me..."

There seems in these lines, to me at least, a sense of stubbornness, that,
although he admits he didn't treat Emma as he should have done, he was
still partially right to, changing, as she had, from "the one who was all to

me." There is some suggestion of blame in this, and it is partly this that makes the poems more human, more engaging. We can all appreciate that Hardy was, like all of us, not perfect, and I find almost universally throughout his writings little reminders of this; certain sentences that are a bit too long, classical references that are a bit too laboured, sentiments that do not exactly cover Hardy with glory. However, these flaws are, as far as I am concerned, like flaws in a precious stone.

The self-reflexiveness of the poems is evidenced not only by his poems about Emma, but also by writing about his childhood, and his memories, even about his parents. For example, "A Church Romance (Mellstock: circa 1835)" details a moment, perhaps even the moment, that his mother and father met, his father playing the 'viol' in church with his mother part of the congregation. It is another example of Hardy's tenderer side, but also of his proclivity to idealise the past. Reading it in tandem with *Under the Greenwood Tree* would provide an appropriate and illuminating point of comparison.

In the novels section of this book (and in this one) I suggested that Hardy does not define his characters in the traditional manner, rather letting them become shaped by the outward processes of Nature and The Immanent Will - like silhouettes. However, with the aforementioned willingness to deal with the self, Hardy's poetry also seemed to allow or encourage him to deal more closely with people, seeing them and their features, rather than just their silhouettes.

"Midnight on the Great Western" gives us an account of a young boy Hardy sees alone on a train one night. We see here both the motif of a journey, a very important image for Hardy, and the motif of the lost boy - one which is not so obvious as the journey, but, still, consciously in his thoughts.

In the third-class seat sat the journeying boy,
And the roof-lamp's oily flame
Played down on his listless form and face,
Bewrapt past knowing to what he was going,
Or whence he came.

In the band of his hat the journeying boy
Had a ticket stuck; and a string
Around his neck bore the key of his box,
That twinkled gleams of the lamp's sad beams
Like a living thing.

What past can be yours, O journeying boy
Towards a world unknown,
Who calmly, as if incurious quite
On all at stake, can undertake
This plunge alone?

Knows your soul a sphere, O journeying boy,
Our rude realms far above,
Whence with spacious vision you mark and mete
This region of sin that you find you in,
But are not of?

On a purely superficial note, nonetheless illustrative of my point, the lamp shining down on the boy - illuminating him, just as Nature might have done in the novels - here does not leave only a silhouette. We can see the details of the boy's figure, the ticket in his hat, the key on a string. In that sense alone, we can tell there is a difference from Hardy's other illustrations of character. As we look further we can see Hardy ask questions directly to and about the boy: *"Knows your soul a sphere…?" "What past can be yours…?"* Hardy seems to show a real interest in this boy, and not the forces that have put him there (The Immanent Will) or what surrounds him (Nature). Again, for a piece of comparative reading, I think it is interesting to look at a copy of William Wordsworth's "Alice Fell". The fact that one of Hardy's poems can be compared with the intensely personal and human-focussed poetry of the Romantics says a lot in itself about this poem.

I began this section with the proposition that the poem "On a Midsummer Eve" gives the reader an encapsulation of Hardy's poetry. I am going to end with a poem which I believe, in a somewhat oblique way, sums up his writing as a whole. "The Darkling Thrush" is, in my opinion, a poem that is immensely suggestive of Hardy's world view.

I leant upon a coppice gate
When Frost was spectre-gray,
And Winter's dregs made desolate
The weakening eye of day.
The tangled bine-stems scored the sky
Like strings of broken lyres,
And all mankind that haunted nigh
Had sought their household fires.

The land's sharp features seemed to be
The Century's corpse outleant,
His crypt the cloudy canopy,
The wind his death-lament.
The ancient pulse of germ and birth
Was shrunken hard and dry,
And every spirit upon earth
Seemed fervourless as I.

At once a voice arose among
The bleak twigs overhead
In a full-hearted evensong
Of joy illimited;
An aged thrush, frail, gaunt, and small,
In blast-beruffled plume,
Had chosen thus to fling his soul
Upon the growing gloom.

So little cause for carolings
Of such ecstatic sound
Was written on terrestrial things
Afar or nigh around,
That I could think there trembled through
His happy good-night air
Some blessed Hope, whereof he knew
And I was unaware.

It begins familiarly with Hardy leaning upon a coppice gate - a support made by rural hands from Nature - with the Frost "spectre-gray". The first stanza sees mankind seeking shelter from Nature's cold and "Winter's dregs." It is also interesting that mankind 'haunts' nigh, rather than 'abides' or 'works' or even 'lives', remembering the mention of ghosts in "On a Midsummer Eve".

The next stanza sees the "Century's corpse outleant," a remnant of the past, now dying, with the current century moving onwards and away from the "ancient pulse of germ and birth," with the advent of mechanisation and industrialisation. Nature is here providing us with reminders of the slow death of the traditional rural way of life which Hardy portrays in his novels; body, crypt, and death lament.

The penultimate stanza brings us relief, or at least so it seems.

The "full-hearted evensong" of "joy illimited" breaks out from the dark, oppressive atmosphere of the preceding stanzas, reminding us of the poet's song who (to quote Auden) "with…[his] unconstraining voice / still persuade[s] us to rejoice." However, "joy illimited" is not exactly what this song provides us with. It should first be noted that the thrush's song is an evensong, from a time not of new birth and growth, but of decay and "growing gloom." Not only this, but the song itself is issuing from "an aged thrush, frail, gaunt, and small, / In blast-beruffled plume." Comparisons can of course be drawn between Hardy and this "aged thrush"; Hardy himself was a man of diminutive stature, and, as photographs reveal, a less than imposing physique. What is also noticeable is that the thrush's song, despite its beauty, does nothing in the grand scheme of things. This again can be said of Hardy; neither *Jude* nor *Tess* changed the way the public thought about marriage or relationships. In this stanza, we see, as in other stanzas, the penultimate line making a reference to ghosts or spirits: "haunted… spirit…soul." This obviously continues the imagery come before, but, where in the previous stanzas Hardy then follows it with a line linking the imagery to the human (where they live, and his own state of 'fervourlesness'), the final line of the stanza leaves us with a definite and conclusive reference to the "growing gloom" of this world. This decline evidences perfectly Hardy's stance as one of the great Victorian pessimists, alongside people like A.E. Housman and Schopenhauer. Though pessimism is most usually what Hardy is associated with, he referred to himself as a 'meliorist'. What that means is that whilst Schopenhauer thought that the world was intrinsically and unalterably a terrible place to live - as bad as it could possibly be - and that it would have all been better if no one was ever born, Hardy believed that the universe was thoroughly bad, but capable of getting better.

Whereas up until the final stanza the world identified by Schopenhauer is prevalent, even dominant, this last verse illustrates the belief of meliorism held by Hardy. Obviously the "blessed hope" whereof Hardy is "unaware" lightens the gloom to an extent; the promise of better things cannot fail to inspire some measure of hope. But, added to that is the unity and continuity of rhythm throughout the poem as a whole. The natural iambic (unstressed-stressed) beat pulses throughout, carrying the message of hope in the shadow of the "growing gloom" until the thrush begins its song, when it peers out tentatively, promising an unidentifiable but nonetheless present force of good.

Lulworth Cove features in Hardy's short story of smuggling "The Distracted Preacher". Hardy's poem "At Lulworth Cove a Century Back" was written to honour John Keats who stopped for a night at Lulworth on his way to Rome in September 1821. Keats had with him one of the last poems he ever wrote "Bright Star, would that I were steadfast as thou are". Hardy mistakenly believed that Keats had written the poem during this brief stop.

Short Stories

Hardy's short stories offer a way into Hardy's world, and exist in a realm different again from his novels and poetry. Whilst his novels were - and it is difficult to deny this - written as part of his job, his poetry was obviously not written with the same economic motive in mind. In stark contrast with the novels, as we have discussed previously, the poems provide the equivalent of an emotional mudslide, nearly burying us in the sentiments and feelings that Hardy perhaps repressed slightly in the novels. In the stories, then, I feel we can see a less obstructed view of Hardy's thoughts - not as militant as *Tess* or *Jude* in espousing beliefs, but more concerned with consideration and exposure of what he saw as problems with the social status quo.

In "The Withered Arm" we have a familiar situation; a woman with a child abandoned by her lover, a young and innocent beauty caught in a web of emotional turmoil she knows nothing about, and, perhaps most noticeably, lashings of dramatic irony. What is different about this story, though, is the lack of an obvious moral or intellectual judgement on the relationships in the plot. In the novels, Jude and Arabella's marriage is seen as unnatural and wrong in the light of Jude's love for Sue, and Tess' connection to Alec is not a natural bond, but a socially contrived and constructed falsity. We do not know the circumstances behind Farmer Lodge's leaving of Rhoda, and so naturally we can't make a judgement. We do get an impression (however vague and familiar) of Gertrude, described as "sweet and kindly," and though we hear that her marriage "sank into prosiness, and worse," there is still little evidence for us to base a judgement on. There is no hint that Farmer Lodge's relationship with Rhoda was in any way superior or inferior to the one with Gertrude. The same is true of the main event of the story - Rhoda's inadvertent wounding of Gertrude. Should we condemn Rhoda for her thoughts, though they were unconscious? Her actions (intended or not) eventually cause Gertrude's death, there is no escaping that. However, Gertrude (again intentionally or not) has displaced Rhoda, and condemned her to a hard, lonely working life, with only her son to keep her company. Looking at it in context with his novels, the previous relationship and new lover are highly suggestive of the two novels mentioned above, both of which favour the new found love over the first as the 'proper' one. But no such clarity exists in "The Withered Arm". A moral judgement on this story, then, is one that has to be made tentatively and with a large amount of personal intuition and feeling, if one needs to be made at all. Thus, the story does not leave us with a militant resounding of the trumpet of Hardy's beliefs, but rather leaves us with a pensive and fuzzy conclusion.

Further showing Hardy's preoccupation with relationships, and how the best ones cannot always thrive in the society Hardy lived in, are three more short stories: "The Distracted Preacher" (of a similar length to "The Withered Arm"), "An Imaginative Woman", and "To Please My Wife" (both notably shorter). There is not enough time here to fully explore the relationships in all three of these, but there is little doubt that each reader may find something different in each of the stories. For instance, in "The Distracted Preacher", we have a priest placed in the unenviable position of having to choose between love and duty - a duty, however, to a social construct which we know Hardy does not think of favourably. This situation, had it occurred in a novel of Hardy's, would almost unquestionably have concluded with a tragic denouement, with society standing in the way of the priest's love for the beautiful smuggler, Lizzy Newberry. However, as with "The Withered Arm", Hardy does not give us, rightly or wrongly, an over-emotional climax - the end is akin to the deflating of a balloon, despite the fact that they, Lizzy and Stockdale, end up married, with Lizzy 'owning that she was wrong' to smuggle. One is certainly left feeling somewhat cheated at the end of the story, but again, it seems as though the short story format allowed Hardy to construct a plot more lucidly, without the cliffhanger endings to each section that serial publication required. It perhaps gives a truer sense of Hardy's idea of a well-constructed story, one without so much of the melodrama necessary to sell it to the general public.

Though this ending seems uncustomary for Hardy, and out of keeping with the sympathetic portrayal of the smugglers in the village, in his old age it seems as though he could not resist either adjusting the story to fit some new-found convictions, or, providing the story with the conclusion he originally wanted:

> "NOTE - The ending of this story with the marriage of Lizzy and the minister was almost de rigueur in an English magazine at the time of writing. But at this late date, thirty years after, it may not be amiss to give the ending that would have been preferred by the writer to the convention used above. Moreover it corresponds more closely with the true incidents of which the tale is a vague and flickering shadow. Lizzy did not, in fact, marry the minister, but - much to her credit in the author's opinion - stuck to Jim the smuggler, and

emigrated with him after their marriage, an expatrial step rather forced upon him by his adventurous antecedents. They both died in Wisconsin between 1850 and 1860.

(May 1912.)"

There is something very mischievous about this appended note, and would suggest that, even when writing short stories, Hardy maybe felt restrained by the reading public as to what he could write. Nonetheless, it is refreshing and not a little enjoyable to see that Hardy could have a bit of fun when he wanted, and didn't spend his whole time imagining the ruin of Michael Henchard and the like.

The two other stories previously mentioned are linked by the fact that they show us two different sides of a marriage. One sees a man bound by duty to a wife who does not really love him, rather than his true love, and who goes to extraordinary lengths to try and make her happy. The other sees a woman yearning for a man other than her husband with whom she feels an instant affinity. The bonds of marriage hold both in an unhappy and unfulfilling relationship, keeping them from who they really want to be with, with both stories ending tragically, or at least unhappily. The ideas in these plots both seem to fall in line with the rest of Hardy's comments on marriage, with "To Please My Wife" ringing with a particularly Hardy-esque tone of bitterness and missed opportunities. But again, as far as I perceive it, evidence in the stories does not signal Hardy coming down unequivocally on one side or the other. It cannot be ignored or forgotten that in "To Please My Wife", the main character and his sons die as a result of the actions of his wife, but it seems to me as though the balance is far more in favour of an admiration and pity of Shadrach Joliffe than condemnation of his union with Joanna. Joliffe is shown as a man of honour and devotion; a simple, honest manifestation of virtues that often appears in Hardy's work, but rarely triumphs. Unsurprisingly, as I have said, Shadrach dies at sea, in search of more wealth with which to appease the shallow and selfish Joanna. Comparisons may certainly be made between the characters of Joliffe and Gabriel Oak, but what is more interesting is whom their devotion was directed to. Oak's to the love of his life, Joliffe's to the woman who stole him away from his true love. Their two different endings certainly suggest a consistency of thought from Hardy, ringing true with ideas formed in his other novels. However, we should note that once again, there is no definite judgement from within the story - the only way we can make an informed guess as to the 'message' of the story is through comparing it with another of Hardy's works, rather than existing in isolation.

"An Imaginative Woman" holds no exception to the moral uncertainties in the aforementioned stories. It is unclear whether blame lies (or indeed should even be involved) with Ella Marchmill for being inconstant to her husband, for not following her heart to Robert Trewe and possibly preventing his death, to William Marchmill for not being what his wife wanted, or even to the young poet for locking himself away from life and potential happiness. A definitive judgement as to Hardy's standpoint is, when looked at in isolation, impossible. What is clear, however, is that Hardy obviously wished to explore the idea of a 'natural' relationship being impeded or prevented by one with a merely social, rather than spiritual, bond.

Although this section contains but a brief reflection on a few of Hardy's stories, the premise of many of them rests on a similar basis, with the same themes occurring again and again. Having said this, though, they rarely get boring, with each one having its own charm and atmosphere. I believe that they are the easiest way into Hardy, both from the point of view of ideas and from a literary point of view.

Right: "Far from the madding crowd...." It is still posssible, in Hardy's Wessex, to find places unchanged since the author's day, and there, perhaps, to appreciate the nature of the influence they had on him. This is the "Abbot's Hospice" at Cerne Abbas [Abbot's Cernel in Hardy's Wessex], part of the old Benedictine abbey that once thrived there. Cerne Abbas featured in "Tess of the D'Urbervilles" and the abbey was the home of the priest sent out onto the wild downland in the poem "The Lost Pyx".

It was not just the romance of such places that influenced Hardy; although now a prosperous village, in Hardy's time Cerne epitomised the hardships of the rural poor. Most people here were farm labourers, their privations made worse by mechanisation and the Inclosure Acts. Testament to this is the large care home on the outskirts of the village, in Hardy's day the local workhouse.

Above: Max Gate, the house that Hardy designed himself. It was built in 1885 and Hardy lived here for the rest of his life.
Below: Hardy with his second wife Florence.

Hardy's Legacy

Hardy's writing is of a truly great importance to the canon of English literature. To count men such as W. H. Auden among the greatest fans of his poetry speaks for itself, as does the incredible staying-power of his novels. But what really makes Hardy both groundbreaking and familiar, but nevertheless loved? The answer, I believe, lies in the previous sentence: Hardy is both groundbreaking (certainly in the history of English literature) in using the pastoral novel as a vehicle for tragedy, and yet the plots, characters and locations often speak with a comforting universality that obscures the unconventional form. The contrasts and contradictions within Hardy's work seem to me to often prevent them from becoming too much of one thing. Hardy paints scenes of stunning scope and width, such as Blackmoor Vale and Egdon Heath, but also has the ability to focus on individuals, dramatically reducing the landscape to a single person, before 'zooming out' again for the wider perspective. Of course, within these descriptions lies part of Hardy's appeal - the sheer beauty of his prose when describing what he knew best.

Furthermore, the way Hardy presents the tragedy or comedy of his characters also creates an engaging play of opposites; when things are going right for a character, Hardy shows it as so finely balanced that the reader is always aware of the possibility for tragedy, and vice versa. It is a curiously masochistic type of enjoyment for the reader, knowing as we do that things cannot remain as they are for long, but it is nonetheless part of Hardy's brilliance. There is another key contradiction in much of Hardy's work that I also see as key to Hardy's appeal. *Jude the Obscure*, for one, is actually set well before its time in order to lend the plot a more convincing air, but the impression one gets from each rural setting in the novels is not one of contemporaneity. As Hardy intimates in *Far from the Madding Crowd*, the country as he sees it is at least twenty, thirty years or more behind the city, and so even reading *The Return of the Native* (for example) on the day it was published would not, I think, have felt like reading about the society and world that the reader was actually living in. For me, this softens any social criticism Hardy may be making in the novels, as at the back of the reader's mind is the sense that the society being accused and the society he or she lives in are not one and the same. This balance between the past and the present is far more pleasant for the reader, and yet does not lose any of the integrity of the message Hardy hoped to convey.

Of course, the whole premise of this book is to provide an introduction to Thomas Hardy and, more particularly, his literary work, not a definitive judgement. This should be left up to the individual. The reader may instead consider that, rather than the constant interplay of contrasts and contradictions being the key factor in Hardy's success, that it was instead his wealth of human experience: his mother and sisters' continuing strong presence in his life; his surprisingly good education; the nature of his surroundings as he grew up; the brutality of the natural and human worlds that he witnessed; Emma, whom he loved and lost, then loved again. Reflecting on each of the above in relation to his writing bears immediate fruit, but still even that does not give a full picture. A good, short introduction to Thomas Hardy's life is Anna Winchcombe's *The Life of Thomas Hardy*; it provides a thorough but relevant overview of significant events in Hardy's life, and is certainly very useful in giving a better context for much of Hardy's work. There is no doubt of the usefulness of context when looking at Hardy's writing.

These reasons hopefully give some idea of why I think Hardy to be worth any attention afforded him by scholars, fans and anybody else willing to abandon themselves to the enchanting innocence and brutal tragedy of his Wessex. He has left us with the possibility for tragedy in the novel, a new style of poetry, one of subtle feelings and simple lexicon in complex forms, and a mythical place created from the ordinary and everyday. Most importantly, he has left us with the impression that literature was not just for the elevated of thought and language, and that he was a writer who had the key commodity of a great writer, something to say.

Acknowledgements

The Dorset County Museum, Dorchester

Front cover photograph and that of Hardy on the title page, Emma p31 and Hardy and Florence p44 are by kind permission of Dorset County Museum who hold the copyright. All other photographs are by Robert Westwood. The museum has a section devoted to Thomas Hardy and a replica of his study at Max Gate. [www.dorsetcountymuseum.org]

The Thomas Hardy Society

The Thomas Hardy Society is based at the Dorset County Museum in Dorchester. Its aim is to promote Hardy's works for "both education and enjoyment" and is for anyone interested in the author at any level. The society has been most helpful and I would particularly like to thank Dee Tolfree for her help and encouragement. [www.hardysociety.org] Tel: 01305 251501

Brief Bibliography

Anna Winchcombe, *The Life of Thomas Hardy*, Dorset Books, Exeter 1989

Claire Tomalin, *Poems of Thomas Hardy*, Penguin, London 2007

Anthony Fincham, "Emma Hardy: The (Mad) Woman in the Attic?", The Thomas Hardy Journal (XXII, pp. 105-128), 2006

Eric Christen, "Hardy in Switzerland: 15 June - 4 July 1897", The Thomas Hardy Journal, (XI, pp. 65-86), 1995

Michael Millgate, "Hardy as Memorialist, The Thomas Hardy Journal", (XV, pp. 65-72), 1999

Stephen Platten, "Hardy's Elusive God, The Thomas Hardy Journal", (XV, pp. 110-112)

Lord David Cecil, *Hardy the Novelist: essays in criticism*, Constable, London 1954

Penelope Vigar, *The Novels of Thomas Hardy: illusion and reality*, Athlone, London 1974

Overleaf: Perhaps Dorset's best known beauty spot - Durdle Door, with Hardy's poem "Nature's Questioning". Hardy's sense of bewilderment with our own (as he sees it) sad state chimes through, but, as often happens, the possible existence of a "Forlorn Hope" shyly peers from the page. This is Hardy at his most typical – questioning, despairing, hoping; all the time letting a rhythmic simplicity hold together the multiple ideas and astute word play.

Nature's Questioning (Wessex Poems and Other Verses, 1898)

WHEN I look forth at dawning, pool,
  Field, flock, and lonely tree,
  All seem to look at me
Like chastened children sitting silent in a school;

Their faces dulled, constrained, and worn,
  As though the master's ways
  Through the long teaching days
Their first terrestrial zest had chilled and overborne.

And on them stirs, in lippings mere
  (As if once clear in call,
  But now scarce breathed at all)—
"We wonder, ever wonder, why we find us here!

"Has some Vast Imbecility,
  Mighty to build and blend,
  But impotent to tend,
Framed us in jest, and left us now to hazardry?

"Or come we of an Automaton
  Unconscious of our pains?…
  Or are we live remains
Of Godhead dying downwards, brain and eye now gone?

"Or is it that some high Plan betides,
  As yet not understood,
  Of Evil stormed by Good,
We the Forlorn Hope over which Achievement strides?"

Thus things around. No answerer I….
  Meanwhile the winds, and rains,
  And Earth's old glooms and pains
Are still the same, and gladdest Life Death neighbors nigh.